What is MonaVie?
What is Acai Berry?
Miracle or Sham?

A Business Analysis and MonaVie Review

Kevin Lindsay

What is MonaVie? What is Acai Berry? Miracle or Sham?

ISBN-13: 978-1483909790

ISBN-10: 1483909794

Table of Contents

Introduction

First, it's important for readers to note that neither I, the author, nor any of my friends or family, have any financial arrangement with the company called MonaVie. I don't market its products, nor am I a distributer, nor will I receive any financial compensation for writing this book from MonaVie.

How this book came about. Originally, I was involved in some in-depth research on the acai berry, finding it to be one of nature's major health miracles. I was so impressed with what the acai berry can do and I was equally amazed at how few people even heard about it. While it had been mentioned by major celebrities from time to time, it is still unknown by the very people that need it most: everyone. It was at the same time that I was reading about network marketing, and how major business names like Donald Trump, Bill Gates, Warren Buffett, etc., were touting it as the perfect method of marketing to bring new ideas into the market place. Especially those that required more time than a 30 second TV advertisement could offer to explain a product's benefits.

I was not so sure. I had heard of pyramid schemes and stories from my father years ago of people having their garages filled with soap. Yet, the more I researched, the more I realized that network marketing would be the perfect way to bring acai berry to the average person. That's when I remembered that I kept running into an acai berry distribution company called MonaVie.

I had not put it together that they were a network marketing company until I did some digging, and what I found was just as amazing as the power of the acai berry itself. I was astonished to discover that MonaVie is without a doubt a vehicle for offering average people an opportunity to build a six or seven figure income and that is only equaled by the power of the acai berry itself to offer the average person a full and healthy life. This book could have been an exposé attacking MonaVie, but instead, it has turned into an honest look at an amazing company with an equally amazing product.

I've divided this book into three parts. First, about the main ingredient of the MonaVie products, acai berry. Second, about

MonaVie itself, and lastly, about network marketing and why no one should have had the resentment I had about it.

Part 1 The Power and Benefits of MonaVie's Acai Berry

What is the truth behind all the hype? Is the Acai berry a miracle food or a lot of talk?

In a world so full of non-natural cures, chemicals and processed foods, cancer causing cosmetic formulations and an eroding and polluted environment, it is rare to see a natural product offer so much to so many people as the Brazilian Acai berry. Once again, nature offers us a perfect medical miracle.

In the past, people could only depend on nature for their food, medicine, clothes and all basic needs. Today, it is no different! People tend to use the fruits and herbs provided by the nurturing earth as food and even for medicinal purposes. The Brazilian Acai berry is just another example of such an offering from the nurturing earth, which has been gaining huge popularity for its use as a healing remedy and for weight loss. They are discovering how the Acai berry is doing powerful things to return people to optimum health, as well as getting them back to their proper weight. The Brazilian Acai berry is a great supplement that you can use to lose weight. Let us go to the history of these berries and understand how they proved so beneficial for health and weight loss.

The fruit originates from a palm tree species, mainly found in floodplains and swamps. A blackish purple round fruit, the Acai berry resembles a grape fruit, but smaller than it, with lesser flesh. Used by the tribal people in the jungles of Amazon, these berries soon became popular for their healing properties for different diseases. It was these tribal people who discovered the qualities of the Acai berry and found that it had the ability to reduce bad cholesterol, strengthen the immune system and provide a lot more benefits, which would be of immense help to mankind.

This extract from the rainforests of Brazil is today well-known for having antioxidants and improving the immune system of humans. Not only does it reduce the amount of bad cholesterol in their body, but its consumption also aids in the increase of the good cholesterol level too, thereby keeping their body in a perfectly healthy condition that is devoid of all excess fats.

For those people who spend hours and hours in a gym or for those who tire themselves out walking long stretches every day, this berry comes as a blessing and a natural means of weight loss, that will work without much effort! While in the past, these berries were more likely to be taken raw, today they come in different forms, including juices and supplements. Juices are the favored methods of delivery, to aid in both absorption and enjoyment.

The berry, also called the "Beauty berry" in Brazil, was found to be full of natural energy and also rich in all proteins, minerals, omega oils and vitamins like Vitamin E, which would help to keep a person's body and immune system under check. It was also known for its ability to control prostate enlargement.

It is also said to offer some similarities to the benefits of Viagra. After the qualities of these berries began to be known to the common man, people, especially the beach boys even began to use the crushed and refrigerated pulp of these berries while enjoying special holidays with their partners!

But the biggest problem in using these berries was that they had a very short lifespan of 24 hours, when the richness and the qualities of the berry would remain. The possibilities of eating the berries raw, so as to take advantage of its qualities, thus became limited, owing to the processes involved in getting the berries from the palms, transportation etc. But soon, researchers found a way to overcome these problems and to make these berries available for us. They developed these berries into a more easily consumable and available form for the market – as Acai berry juices and supplements.

Coming in the form of juices, these berries have the power not only to boost your immunity but also to fight infections and to provide protection to your heart. Now, you may be wondering how can such a product help reduce heart disease. The fact is that the ratio of fatty acids in the Acai berry is almost similar to that of olive oil, which is well known for its ability to control heart disease, over normal oils. This is the same reason why the juices made from these berries can help you keep your heart protected.

Deb, like most faithful Monavie users, has been overweight all of her life. After trying hundreds of diets, she realized the routine: lose some weight, then gain it back. Sometimes gaining more weight than she had to begin with. However, MonaVie RVL has been different; this is the plan that has made her feel and look good, and has been easy to maintain. She started the diet on November 8th, 2010 and lost fifty pounds in nine months. She proudly states that she is fifty-five years old and now she "feels better than I ever have in my life." That is what MonaVie does--it lets that ideal you that you've always dreamed of come out, and shine.

Studies also indicate that the Acai berry has the ability to fight and kill cancer cells, due to the fact that it is one of the best antioxidant berries available today, even stronger than ginkgo biloba, which had been known for its high medicinal properties for more than a thousand years. They can extrapolate that by consuming Acai berry juice, you are not just making your immune system stronger, but you are making yourself less prone to deadly cancers! They will read about the research behind this extrapolation later in the book.

Today, acai berry juices are highly popular among the stars as well as average people, as a simple means of weight loss and in keeping the immune system strong so they stay protected from diseases.

There are a lot of products available on the market today with the Acai berry as their main ingredient. The MonaVie Acai berry juice is one such supplement that is very popular. Studies reveal that the MonaVie Acai berry juice is currently being used by many Hollywood stars and individuals from all over the world who are trying to lose weight and stay healthy in a safe and effective manner.

Weight loss without working out? Can that even be possible?

Now that they have gone through the history and details of the Acai berry and the juice supplements that contain their extracts, let's examine some more details about how amazing berry works to reduce weight and boost your immune system.

Scientists and Doctors call the Acai berry a super-food. This is because it consists of a whole lot of nutrients, minerals, and vitamins which help in managing the whole of your body well enough to keep it healthy and young. The Acai berry is known to consist of natural ingredients that boost your metabolic rate. A boost in the metabolic rate of your body can cause the use of more calories to get your daily tasks done. This, in turn, results in your body burning excess fat faster.

The fiber content in these supplements also tends to reduce your craving of eating, by giving you a feeling of a full stomach. The reduced intake of food also helps in reducing the weight of the body by a good amount.

Studies reveal that the antioxidants in Acai berries cleanses your body, kidneys and liver from any toxic materials that you may have consumed, thereby making your body stronger and resistant to diseases. Some of these antioxidants include anthocyanins and homoorientin.

Now how do these toxic substances enter your body? The fact is that your normal metabolic activities can cause the formation of some toxic substances within the body. Along with this, exposure to cigarette smoke, polluted air etc. can also result in the inhalation of toxic substances as well. These substances cause the formation of free radicals, which in turn leads to degeneration of their cells, causing damages and diseases. The strong antioxidants in the Acai berry allow more flow of oxygen into the body and destroy these free radicals, thereby making cell growth possible. This in turn makes you stronger and tougher against all diseases.

Apart from this, the berry is known to consist of rare nutrients and monounsaturated fats. They are also one of the few fruits that contain these unique types of fats. It is a well-known fact that mono-unsaturated fats are very beneficial when it comes to dieting and losing weight quickly. Acai berries consist of several nutrients such as iron, calcium, and even different vitamins that are vital for the body, including Vitamin A, Vitamin C etc., which promotes betterment of the skin, enhanced vision and so many more qualities that help to keep you younger and more active, even at old age!

After the advantages of using the Acai berry started to gain popularity, several researches and studies were conducted on it, to prove the antioxidant abilities of the berry in fighting cancer cells, increasing the energy level of the body etc. And miraculously, these studies and researches conducted helped to show the fact that Acai berries possess the ability to destroy dangerous cancer cells, provide more energy to the body and boost one's immune system.

In the year 2006, Florida University conducted a research on the abilities of the Acai berry to kill cancer causing cells. The university was one among the first to research the advantages of the Acai berry. The experienced personnel of the University including Stephen Talcott, Susan Percival and David Del conducted the researches on the Acai berry and its cancer killing abilities. The research was conducted on cultured cancer cells and it was found that after the use of the berries on these cancer cells, the cells began to die. Talcott described this study as an important part in learning how these Acai juice and the berries themselves can be of use to the mankind.

But these results weren't completely backed by the researchers. This was because the research was done on cultured cancer cells and not real ones. And for this reason, the researchers did not wish to spread a false hope about a natural treatment for this disastrous disease! Moreover, the study pointed to the fact that the effect of such antioxidants on the growth of cancer cells were influenced by many other factors, like the metabolism rate, nutrient absorption etc. Hence, coming to a complete conclusion that the Acai berries can prevent the attack of cancer fully became quite plausible, but not proven. Reports from those who take the juice and had fought cancer have supported this very plausible conclusion.

Amber is both a dancer and a dance teacher and has spent her entire life as the athletic girl in the room, but since she had a baby girl in 2007 she has been stuck with an extra ten pounds she felt she would never get rid of. She explains that she would dance for hours, run three miles a day pushing a stroller up hill, and the weight was resistant--she was at a plateau. Then, in 2010, she had a baby boy. She had this pregnancy weight to lose now, in addition to the stubborn ten pounds her girl left. Everyone always told her that your body is never the same after you have kids, and she believed them. Amber's hope diminished. She began the Monavie program in November and by February she defeated the plateau to drop from 115 lbs. to 110, which she has since healthfully maintained. She has finally lost that baby belly, she excitedly announces. With the weight loss, she reports a massive gain of energy, which she needs to handle these two kids. "I don't think I will ever go a day without my MonaVie RVL shake," she states, explaining that it so greatly improves both her health and her mood. She weighs now what she did as a teenager, but now has a lot more confidence. She is ready to face bikini season, her MonaVie in hand!

The University of Florida also conducted another research towards the end of 2006, regarding the antioxidant effect of the Acai berries on healthy individuals. The intention of this study was to understand the rate at which the blood absorbs the compounds, and their effects on the cholesterol levels, blood pressure etc. of a person.

In 2008, a study was conducted by the University of Texas to examine the health benefits of acai berry. Twelve healthy volunteers were chosen and were asked to consume just one serving of the Acai berry in pulp or juice form. Urine and blood samples were then taken from all the volunteers after a break of 12 hours and 24 hours.

It was found that all the volunteers experienced an increase in their antioxidant activity and an improvement in their immunity system. Studies are still being conducted on the benefits of the Acai berries and the other qualities it may possess, which in turn can be a break-through in the treatment of several diseases and ailments.

The Ultimate 11 Benefits of the Brazilian Acai berry you need to know

1 A part from what was stated above, Acai has very few or no side effects whatsoever. The fact remains that it is a simple berry available naturally from the forests. Studies reveal that these berries were in use hundreds of years ago as a means of increasing one's energy level and even as a cure from many diseases. The fact that these berries can be taken fresh or in the pulped form or even as juices, without adding any chemical to them supports the statement that there are very few or no side effects at all for these berries or supplements made from them.

2 Enables you to lose weight easily – For those people who are tired of spending countless hours in their life, trying to burn out the excess fat in your body, Acai berry juice would be worth trying. Instead of spending long hours doing exercises, often a person just need to make the Acai berries or its juice a mandatory part of their daily diet. The ability of the Acai berry to limit the conversion of the carbohydrates consumed into body fat is the main aid in keeping body weight under control.

This supplement tends to stabilize blood sugar and bring down the bad cholesterol in their body, while promoting the increase in good cholesterol level. Moreover, they increase metabolism rate, which causes the use of more calories to burn in their body daily. This, in turn, helps a person to lose weight and keep their body weight under check, that too, without much effort! The role of the fiber contained in the Acai berry juice should also not be overlooked. The contents when eaten, tend to fill your stomach to satisfaction, which in turn reduces the amount of food consumed for a day. That is, it acts as a hunger suppressant. And that, of course, aids in quick weight loss!

3 Slows down aging – The Acai berries have not only been known for their weight loss properties, but they have also been well-known from long ago for their ability to bring about youthfulness to one's skin. The women and men of years ago used to eat these berries to keep themselves fresh and young. The fact is that these berries aided in increasing one's sexual desire, something that keeps a human being full of life, no matter what age he or she is!

Moreover, the anti-oxidant properties of the berries made them the best choice in the search for a natural anti-aging product. One of the main anti-oxidants in the Acai Berry, called anthocyanins, is expected to be the cause of the anti-aging properties of the Acai berry. Today, these berries are being used not only in diet supplements but also in beauty products, including anti-aging creams and other cosmetic items, owing to the anti-aging properties they possess.

How exactly do they slow down aging? These berries are rich in flavonoids, which help in fighting inflammations. They also have fatty acids, amino acids etc., which act with these flavonoids to aid in the regenerative growth of one's skin cells. Moreover, these berries contain a significant amount of nutrients that help to keep one's skin and body healthy and glowing. It is not just about slowing down aging. These berries in the beauty products help to absorb moisture into your skin and aid in the removal of blemishes, skin infections etc., which in turn helps to give a better tone to your skin. It is even said to protect you from the harmful UV rays of the sun as well as other stressors that might harm your skin and cause quick aging.

Carina writes in that she and her husband both started the MonaVie RVL program in November, following the basic guidelines of consuming two shakes, two snacks, and a healthy meal every day, as well as the Monavie Active. She explains that she loved the transition from the beginning; "I was satisfied and I never felt hungry or weak," she explains. She was able to continue donating blood, despite the change. Carina developed a fitness routine of walking, light hiking, and recently tennis as well, and has seen a loss of 23 pounds and 22 inches already, after just a handful of months on the program. Carina is a rarity--this is her very first weight loss program--and she couldn't be happier with the results. She proclaims proudly, "MonaVie RVL truly values life through healthy weight loss."

4 Enhanced cardiovascular health – The Acai berry juices are known to have the ability to protect your heart from diseases and keep it healthy. How is this achieved? The main reason for this is the fact that the juices contain a lot of minute ingredients that can directly and indirectly aid in protecting your heart. The health of your heart has a lot to do with the level of fats and cholesterol in your body. With its beneficial properties that aid in the reduction of bad

cholesterol and burning of calories, Acai berry juice reduce the chances of a person to be prone to heart diseases and other cardio-vascular problems. The berries and its juice also have the ability to reduce the blood pressure of your body. Studies reveal that taking the Acai berry juice can bring down your chances of suffering from a stroke by a huge percentage.

5 Enhances the digestion process – The ability of Acai berry juice to speed up the metabolism of the human body is the secret behind this. The fatty acids, omega acids etc. present in the Acai berries aid in better metabolic rates and along with this, causes the speeding up of the digestion of food that is being consumed.

6 Improves blood circulation and cholesterol levels – Due to the ability of the Acai berries to vary the cholesterol level in the body. Juices containing the Acai berry also have this same healthy benefit. The reduction in the amount of bad cholesterol and the increase in the amount of good cholesterol in the body help in keeping the cholesterol levels at check and preventing excess fats in getting deposited in the body. The nutrients, minerals etc. present in the berry are the major contributors of increased blood circulation throughout their body, which in turn, leads to an increase in their total energy level, at no matter what age! Moreover, these juices tend to detoxify and clean up their system, thereby making their body better and healthier in all manner of ways.

7 Decreases joint pain – This is very beneficial for individuals who suffer from arthritis and other similar problems. How is this achieved? As mentioned above, these supplements aid in better circulation of the blood throughout the body, which in turn helps in relaxing your muscles and reducing joint pains. For those who have constant joint pains, muscle pains etc., the Acai berry juice can turn out to be a good medicine that gives relief from their constant pains. Taking this juice will also improve the condition of your muscles and enhance the process of muscle regeneration, which is great for body builders and those who exercise.

8 Improves sex drive – Sex drive is something that keeps a man and woman young and fresh, no matter what age they are. It is a known fact that the sex drive decreases in most people, with the increase in age and this is one of the major reasons that cause you to look aged physically. Even from ancient times, the Acai berry was known to have a good effect on the sexual desire of a human being.

Studies revealed that taking the pulp of these berries could help in enhancing your sex drive regardless of your age. Today the Acai berry juices is being used not only as a means of weight loss but also secretly to increase sex drive and bring about a better interest in one's partner. This has particularly been very beneficial for those individuals who have an unstable sexual relationship with their partner and those people who have been experiencing trouble in their married life.

9 Boost to your immune system – Resistance to diseases is something they all possess right from the time they are born. But the level of immunity in each individual may vary according his body, eating habits etc. The Acai berry juices are said to be the best friends of those people who have a weak immune system. Why is the Acai berry good for your immune system?

Studies reveal that the Acai berries grew in tough conditions and were exposed to a lot of sunlight, due to the height of the Acai palms. So as to overcome the harmful effects of sunrays, Nature itself is said to have given these berries a huge supply of antioxidants which would provide more oxygen and would help the berry exist in these tough conditions. The anti-oxidant powers of the berries are suspected to be the real causes to the boost in the immune system of the person eating them. It has been found that these anti-oxidants in the Acai berries have the strong ability to destroy or kill the free radicals and aid in the healing of any damaged cell in the human body. Hence, the Acai berry diet supplements are also said to possess these powers of strengthening your immune system and making you less prone to diseases, unlike many other health supplements.

10 Ability to fight cancer cells – As mentioned before, the strong anti-oxidant properties of the Acai berry supplements are said to aid in destroying cancer cells to an extent. The berries are known to have 5 times better anti-oxidant properties compared to the best anti-oxidants known to man today and this is expected to become a breakthrough in the treatment of cancer, according to continuing studies. Although research is being conducted on this and a clear statement is not yet possible that these supplements can prevent cancer from attacking a human body completely, it may soon come. Better safe than sorry so take them now. They can only help.

Efrain has struggled with being overweight since he was a child, typically finding poor results with diets and products, and the occasional very temporary success, met with more failure. He started the MonaVie RVL program in November of 2010 and says that not only is he now seeing great success, but he's reaching this success in a healthy way. Efrain explains that this amazing product has changed his life --he can tie his own shoes now, and is able to hug and dance with his wife without his belly being in the way. For his fresh new energy and new enjoyment in waking up to exercise, he praises Monavie.

After extensive research and study, I have found that MonaVie is a company that values its products as much as its customers and clients. MonaVie realizes that everyone around the world suffers in some way from various health issues. From lighter health issues to those that are more pressing matters, I have seen conclusive evidence that MonaVie does its best to ensure that people are receiving solutions to whatever health problems ail them, as best that it can.

MonaVie's commitment to excellence is what has made it the fastest growing company in the Inc. 500 Food and Beverage category after only five years of business. MonaVie juice was first released in January of 2005 by Monarch Health Sciences, which itself was founded in 2003 in order to distribute various dietary and weight loss products. Later that year, the executives of Monarch Health Services saw the true potential of MonaVie and decided to open MonaVie as its own privately held company. Both companies were founded in Salt Lake City, Utah, by Dallin Larsen, who is the current Chairman of the Board at MonaVie.

Dallin Larsen has been working in direct sales for over two decades, during which he has also been working with various nutritional and dietary products. An entrepreneur from the beginning, Dallin Larsen was able to put himself through Brigham Young University in Provo, Utah, by opening a chain of shaved ice shacks all over the state of Utah. By the end, they had twenty shaved ice shacks open and running throughout the state. At the age of 22, Dallin Larsen convinced his family to invest in the weight-loss franchise Diet Center. After convincing his father to cosign a loan to open his first franchise, Dallin Larsen succeed in opening four more franchises. This was no doubt where he learned how to hire people and run a business, but his experience running Diet Center franchises also taught him that much of the success that a business sees is due to the people who work there.

In the late 1980s, a friend introduced Dallin Larsen to the idea of network marketing. In other words, he became a distributer for a 'multi-level marketing' company. From the get-go, the concepts of network marketing and running a company through distributers intrigued him. Later, when he met the founder of Usana, a network marketing company that works with nutritional products, he was asked to join their team. For nine years, Dallin Larsen worked with Usana and grew the company to over a hundred million dollars in sales.

In 2003, Dallin Larsen joined forces with four-time Olympian Henry Marsh to start Monarch Health Science, a weight-loss company. Off to a rocky start, the company did not see much success. Then, Dallin Larsen heard about the acai berry. Nicholas Perricone, a world-famous doctor, had even gone on The Oprah Winfrey Show to talk about the acai berry being one of the world's greatest superfoods. The acai berry was said to be filled to the brim with nutritional value. After doing some research, he asked one of the scientists of Monarch Health Science to do further tests and find out more about this miracle berry. After blending the berry with nineteen other fruits, the company introduced MonaVie.

MonaVie hit the market and spread like wildfire. A distributer in Florida introduced MonaVie to Sumner Redstone, the chairman of

Viacom, and he was hooked. A short time later, the product was featured in Fortune magazine. It even became the official team juice of the Boston Red Sox after players J.D. Drew and Jonathan Papelbon became avid supporters of the juice and voiced their love for it. The company has grown a great deal since 2003 and even had a car racing in the Indy 500 in 2009 to launch their energy drink.

Julie had stage four cancer three years ago, and says that she began taking Monavie immediately after she went into remission. This product has replenished her energy levels and cured all of her joint pain. She cites Dr. Alexander Schauss, director of Natural and Medicinal Products Research for AIBMR Life Sciences in Washington, who has studied nutrition and botanical medicine for over three decades, as a great source on Monavie. He has written that the fruits in Monavie possess vital nutrients that improve our health that have earned an ORAC score (measuring antioxidant content) at over ten times higher than any other food ever tested by the USDA. Julie specifically cites "The Perricone Promise" and "Ultimate Anti-Aging Checklist" and any other article by Dr. Schauss on the acai berry or other fruits in Monavie, a true miracle product.

Track-and-field Olympian Henry Marsh set four records during his career in America and was ranked number one in the world for three years. His experience as an athlete as well as with the President's Council on Physical Fitness and Sports, the executive board for the United States Olympic Committee, and as a member of the board of trustees for the Salt Lake City Olympic Committee during the Winter Games of 2002 have contributed greatly to his success in the industry of the distribution of nutritional products. He is now working as one of the founders and a Vice Chairman of MonaVie, where he puts his experience as an athlete, as well as his degrees in Law and Economics, to very good use.

While Henry Marsh was never able to capture the gold at the Olympics thanks in part to a series of poorly timed boycotts, falls, and illnesses, everything that he's dabbled in since then has become far more valuable.

Randy Larsen, brother of Dallin Larsen, has played a great role in MonaVie as well. In addition to serving as the first Chief Operating Officer of MonaVie, Randy Larsen was able to negotiate the first acai deal, bringing super berry to the company for the first time. Randy has played an important role in establishing MonaVie's main business functions, which includes the sustainable harvesting program for procuring the acai berries from the Amazon Rainforest. This program provides employment to hundreds of families who live along the Amazon River and consistently works to save the rainforest.

Randy Larsen, like his brother, has a history of working as a successful entrepreneur. He has owned and operated retail chains, restaurants, and an assortment of small businesses all over the United States. While working MonaVie, he also serves as a board member for several other companies. Randy Larsen has also been an active member in the development of nutritional products for over twenty-five years and has worked in the direct-selling industry for sixteen-plus years. Randy Larson currently serves as President over the MonaVie markets in the Asia Pacific region.

The experience of these three men and knowledge in these fields as well as the professional insight that they have brought to the table have helped to make MonaVie the number one fastest growing company in Utah. With Dallin Larsen at the helm of the company, MonaVie was able to achieve the aforementioned number one fastest growing company in the Inc. 500 Food and Beverage category. After only five years of business, Dallin Larsen already had MonaVie rising straight to the top.

The success of MonaVie is due not only to the prowess of Dallin Larsen but to the distributers who worked directly with the MonaVie product line. Dallin Larsen recognizes the contribution of each distributer who works with MonaVie, and his love and appreciation for them has been the prime driving force behind the company's reputation for putting its distributers first. Keeping this philosophy in mind is why Dallin Larsen has seen so much unprecedented success in such a short amount of time. His philosophy and dedication to the company have also earned Dallin Larsen the recognition of being named a 2009 Ernst and Young Entrepreneur of the Year Award Winner as well as the 2010 Utah Business magazine CEO of the Year.

Over a million distributers have already been enrolled in MonaVie, and that number is constantly climbing higher and higher. MonaVie was designed so that a distributer doesn't need to be a superhero to achieve success. Unlike other companies that use distributers as the main channel for their product distribution, MonaVie was set up so that distributers don't have to go knocking on every door they see or stock up on thousands of dollars' worth of the product in order to see a profit.

Other companies in the industry of network marketing might not be legitimate, but the business idea itself is over a hundred years old. Even celebrities such as Warren Buffet have invested in direct-selling companies. Oftentimes, the companies that have made people wary or cautious about the idea of network marketing or even working as a distributer for such a company have had a faulty or illegitimate product. Many of those companies have been rightfully shut down. Dallin Larsen and everyone at MonaVie, on the other hand, make sure that MonaVie operates in an extraordinary manner where the products are properly backed up and the distributers aren't making extreme claims about MonaVie or its products.

Because MonaVie has seen such great success, people from all over the world are calling to find out more about the products and work to expand the company internationally. In fact, in 2009, MonaVie began selling its products in over twenty countries outside of the United States. MonaVie's international growth has seen great success and so have the distributers working with the company. The top earners at MonaVie make over five million dollars a year, proving that they are indeed very productive people.

What are MonaVie's goals?

MonaVie's goal is not to be the best company in the world. MonaVie's goal is to be the best company FOR the world. MonaVie wants to help the world not only through its products but also through any way possible and by any means necessary. The MORE Project was founded by Dallin Larsen, his brother Randy Larsen, and Henry Marsh to feed, clothe, and educate the children and adults living in the slums of Brazil.

These men, as the founders of MonaVie, wanted to run a company that was able to give back to the world. They worked together to foster a corporate culture in the company that valued charity as a principle governing the actions of both the distributers and the employees. They were extremely successful, and that is how the MORE Project came into existence. MonaVie's incredible growth from the company's beginning fueled the founders' sense of urgency to partner with a non-profit organization that was capable of truly making a difference in children's lives.

Doug Rowland, a MonaVie distributer who had done his own charity work in Brazil, stepped up and introduced them to Sergio Ponce, who had established a project of his own on the outskirts of Rio de Janeiro. Sergio Ponce's love and commitment to the people living in the favelas of Brazil impressed Dallin Larsen to the point that he and his wife decided to support the project and set it up as an independent non-profit organization. The MORE Project was founded by MonaVie, which has played an integral role in supporting the MORE Project's growth and stability by making it one of the five stars of the MonaVie business plan. The MORE Project is the cause that drives MonaVie. MonaVie actively funds the administrative costs of the MORE Project so that those who make donations to the organization know that their money goes directly to those who really need it. The MORE Project will continue to run with the support of MonaVie until it is able to finish what it has started.

MonaVie has tried to maintain a low profile, but the success of its products over the years has brought it into the mainstream on more than one occasion. Through its charitable actions, celebrity endorsements, and overall great products, MonaVie has become a well-known company. As previously mentioned, MonaVie is a company that relies on community commerce, otherwise known as direct sales, to move its products.

Community commerce is some of the most powerful marketing that exists in the world. What kind of recommendation are you more likely to act on: a personal recommendation or one that comes directly from a company? This is nothing new to the world, though. Before people were constantly attacked by advertisements on radio, TV, or the Internet, people and companies of all sizes relied heavily on word of mouth.

MonaVie believes in giving people the power to change their own lives by working as distributers and earning money for themselves. They believe that empowering their distributers can bring their happiness and stability into reach. Regardless of whether you've decided that you're ready to make a change that will improve your personal circumstances, improve the health of the ones that you love, or significantly change your life for the better, MonaVie is here with an opportunity that will allow you to make your mark in the constantly growing health and wellness industry.

Gina has suffered from Meneire's Disease with serious vertigo for a while but since beginning Monavie three months ago she hasn't experienced any form of dizziness. She received the product through her cousin and proudly proclaims that she promotes the product whenever possible. At a recent appointment her doctor noticed a drop in blood pressure and cholesterol and said that whatever she's doing differently, "don't stop!" A positive result seen by the patient and doctor alike is a major win in my book.

MonaVie's independent distributers are entrepreneurs with amazing products. They have the support of a large support staff and marketing team, an extremely friendly customer support team, and a very distinguished research and development team backing them up. Add to that the fact that MonaVie keeps coming out with new products makes the job of a MonaVie distributer very simple. MonaVie has the tools for their distributers to use to determine whatever success means to you and to help you achieve it. As one of their distributers, you'll be able to show your pride and offer fantastic products that offer the power of antioxidants and weight management solutions. You will also have the backing of everyone at MonaVie to aid in achieving your goals.

How does MonaVie continue to compete?

Health and wellness has become a multi-billion dollar industry over the past few decades, so there is no surprise in seeing hundreds of new products hitting the markets and springing up all over the world. MonaVie has seen success in every market that it has entered and will continue to grow around that world as it moves into new countries.

MonaVie offers a variety of very popular and healthy products, particularly products that work to prevent cardiovascular diseases and keep those who live in warmer climates with a lot of UV exposure looking younger and healthier.

The profit that comes from helping others

Once you've learned about the products, you'll see why Mona-Vie has become one of the fastest growing companies in the history of community commerce. MonaVie is without a doubt the number one community commerce opportunity open to the public today. MonaVie employs the most innovative and dynamic compensation plan that the community commerce industry has ever seen, so there's no reason to wonder how or why MonaVie is fostering health, wealth, and happiness in cities all around the world.

There are ten ways to earn income, and fifty percent of the sales volume is regularly paid out in distributer commissions. MonaVie is an incredibly rewarding and sustainable opportunity for those who wish to come aboard and start their own business.

The great thing about MonaVie's unique style of community commerce is that it can work no matter where you are or what your circumstances might be. MonaVie distributers who have found success are professionals such as doctors, educators, and lawyers of all kinds. Some of their distributers are stay-at-home moms or dads who are working with MonaVie to supplement or replace income that is lost. Other distributers never had the chance to receive an education but have the intelligence and guts to create a successful business and improve the lives of their loved ones and children. They even have distributers who are living in third world countries and are finding that MonaVie is one of the greatest business opportunities that has ever come their way.

That's the kind of community commerce that they've worked to create at MonaVie. It fosters the type of opportunity and success that over a billion people all over the world who are either unemployed or underemployed are looking for. When you buy and consume MonaVie products, your health and well-being will both benefit. When you move a step forward and recommend these products to others, you create a residual income that might even outlive you.

When you join the MonaVie team, you'll join the likes of PGA Golfer Bo Van Pelt who says, "MonaVie is an once-in-a-lifetime opportunity that combines an amazing product and a wonderful cause with a rewarding business plan. They have a blast sharing MonaVie and look forward to a bright future."

Professional Sports Photographer Tom DiPace is also a great part of the MonaVie team. "I enjoy success with MonaVie using the same people skills I developed in my photography career – relationship marketing!" If you think you have the skills to be a great distributer, MonaVie has the right product for you.

What are the necessary requirements for success in MonaVie?

As a distributer, you might face a lot of no's from customers or clients. You'll hear a lot of reasons that people can't take the product, and you'll want to offer them the reasons as to why the product is right for them. MonaVie does not want its distributers to do that in a sleazy way. Passion for the product is what creates the ability to meet a customer or client's needs on the scene and make a deal. MonaVie provides a variety of great products that you will have no problem representing.

With the backing of your support team at head office and an amazing product to sell, passion for MonaVie's products comes easy and enables you to sell a product that you can be proud of and that you can believe in.

Some of the distributers who are the most successful are the ones who are willing to listen closely to their customers and clients. One thing that they focus on at MonaVie is knowing what people like and what people want. As long as you're listening to your customers and clients, you'll be able to find that MonaVie products are just what they're looking for, regardless of whether or not they already know it. The team at MonaVie works to ensure that only the best products will reach your customers and clients so that you can use your listening skills to hear how great they are!

Joe reports that he has had Rheumatoid Arthritis since he was thirty, and after eight years on Hydrocychloroquine and steroids he felt dejected about the heavy dose of medicine. He began taking Monavie and, after just three weeks, he is able to spend his mornings and long weekends doing yard work without much pain at all. He owes this minor but meaningful success to Monavie.

These days, head office people at MonaVie know that their newest distributers are no strangers to questioning what's possible. After all, you wouldn't be here if you weren't eager or willing to try something new. Because of this, they know that their distributers are already able to understand their customers. MonaVie offers a variety of products that will appeal to people of any and all backgrounds, so their distributers need to know who they're selling which product to. While a juice might appeal to a customer looking for a delicious and healthy drink, their Active Gel might appeal to a more athletic customer or client who needs the energy to stay active longer. MonaVie wants their distributers to know that being able to understand and adapt to each client is a very important quality that will help them do very well while working with them.

At MonaVie, they don't expect all of their distributers to be athletes or nutrition experts, but they do expect them to embody their company culture. They believe in making the world a better place, and it is very important that they as well as their distributers remember that they are working not only for themselves but to help people all around the world.

Think back to the MORE project and everything that it does to help adults and children alike who need the opportunity for a better life. A good distributer will use this to fuel their passion for MonaVie and the uniqueness of their products. That passion should also come with great execution. Their customers and clients should never be left wondering whether or not their distributer will come through. At MonaVie, they do what they say they will do and deliver what they say they will deliver.

To expand on that, their ideal distributers are somebody's best friend. In this case, the somebody is your customer or client. In community commerce, people will learn about you as a distributer from their friends that you have done business with already, not from an advertisement. Because of this, it's important to be reliable and trusted by your customers and clients. If you're able to befriend one client, that client might introduce you to his or her circle of friends who are interested in doing business with you, too. They don't want their distributers merely to treat their customers and clients as acquaintances; they want them to be friends.

With their products, MonaVie doesn't try to create a lot of mystery around their products. There's a clear science to making their products and research to back it up. Their best distributers are knowledgeable about their product lines and have the ability to talk about those products and that science in terms that will translate easily to the average person. Once you're able to explain what the product is and why it will help, all you have to do as one of their distributers is get the order and collect payment.

MonaVie wants their distributers to have great follow-through and customer service. All over the world, customers and clients expect great customer service, so don't just say it; do it. This level of customer service can come from a variety of methods. You can send thank-you notes, make courtesy check-in calls, and respond quickly to client requests with a smile on your face. As often as possible, they at MonaVie try to anticipate the needs of their customers before they make a request. Remember, sometimes a mistake can be a distributer's best friend. React quickly and make things right with integrity, and you can elevate yourself, their products, and their brand in the eyes of that client or customer.

One thing you can always remember while you're working with MonaVie is that you'll never have to go it alone. When you work with MonaVie, you have a team within the organization that will help you. That is their job. Just like someone climbing Mount Everest will seek the advice of a Sherpa, you, too, should seek the advice and support of their team. The best distributers are those who can work with an internal system. Use their team to facilitate higher dialogue with hard-to-get customers; collaborate with your marketing and sales team to learn from their efforts and support their best strategies; and never be afraid to ask someone for help if you feel as though you are losing ground with a prospective client.

New Trends in Networking and Community Commerce

The method by which distributers move products in community commerce has gone through massive changes over the past few decades, and the entire process has gone from a one-way "push the benefits" model to an in-depth, online research analysis on the part of the customer long before they might even interact with a distributer.

Today's customers will conduct research about their products online to find out more about their products, services, and maybe even information about you on a personal level. Their distributers should keep this in mind and try to maintain a positive online presence so that present and future clients are never disappointed with what they find.

By this time, you have read quite a bit about their company and what they have to offer. You've learned a lot about where Mona-Vie has come from, who they have worked with, and the kind of person that they like to work with. The only question now is are you ready?

MonaVie offers a great, innovative, and unique compensation plan to its distributers and is always ready to welcome new people on board. If you think you have what it takes to become a distributer or even open a franchise of your own, they urge you to reach out to MonaVie today.

Keep your integrity, reach out to the person who first showed you the MonaVie business, and get going.

Stephanie explains that her husband, the father of her two children, missed out a lot on their childhoods due to intense pain and a high dose of daily medication due to scar tissue strangling his sciatic nerve. After three bottles of Monavie he requested his doctor to reduce his prescription of morphine. Since three days on this juice he hasn't asked for his meds to be increased, which used to be a daily occurrence. "Try tell him it's a crock!" she demands about Monavie. This product has changed his life.

If you're ready to join the fastest growing community commerce company in the world, they're ready to welcome you to the team. MonaVie has blueprints laid out with the intention of continuing expansion within the United States as well as markets worldwide. Suffice to say, they have some big plans. MonaVie is helping people around the world with many different backgrounds to achieve their own view of success. Their goal isn't merely to sell a product; their goal is to relieve the hopelessness that plagues this world and to be the strong hand that lifts people form the ground so that they can stand on their own two feet.

The success of MonaVie isn't theirs alone. It's all about their independent distributers sharing great products and making money for a better well-being. Whether you're looking to significantly transform your life or for a way to add more money to your current income, you can join the hundreds of thousands of successful distributers in redefining their lives with top-notch nutritional products and effective weight loss solutions.

MonaVie's Product Line and the Science

At MonaVie, their researchers and scientist are constantly working on unlocking, sharing, and protecting Earth's most unique, helpful resources. They combine science and nature to bring their customers the best quality products that they are able to produce.

To date, they have drawn upon millions of dollars to spend on clinical research alone. Their products have been supported by over 60 independently run scientific studies. MonaVie scientists have also had ten studies published in national, peer-reviewed journals and hold 4 patents in the United States.

Their company is dedicated to the health of the world and everyone who lives in it, but their dedication doesn't end there. They are constantly working and running clinical research to improve the products that they've already produced as well as create new products that will be beneficial to their customers.

The Science

Many people have heard about antioxidants, but not everyone knows what they do. Their bodies are like battlegrounds where they fight against infection and various diseases. Oxygen is essential to all life as they know it, but it can also be detrimental to your health. While your body's cells create energy using oxygen, they also create a byproduct called free radicals, which can potentially cause damage.

What Are Free Radicals?

Free radicals are atoms that have an electron in their outer cellular ring that is not part of a pair. Because electrons generally exist in pairs, free radicals tend to become unstable and connect to electrons from other atoms and molecules in the body. This cycle creates a chain reaction in your body that can cause damage to cell membranes, accelerate the aging process, and contribute to a number of different illnesses. Many things can contribute to the production and formation of free radicals, including stress, UV radiation, pollution, exercise, lack of sleep, and stress.

These unstable free radicals can cause oxidative stress, which is an imbalance in your body. When this imbalance occurs, the body is not able to counter the damage done by the free radicals. If you want to see it in action, cut an apple in half. Once the fruit is exposed to air, its starts to turn brown. The oxygen in the air is interacting within the cell wall, creating free radicals in the apple's tissues. Oxidative stress can cause damage to DNA, proteins, and other macromolecules that can lead to a range of human diseases, including heart disease and cancer as well as a decline in the function of the brain and the immune system. Spread a little lemon juice or Mona-Vie juice on the other side of the cut apple, and notice it does not turn brown. This is the power of antioxidants.

Generally speaking, free radical formation is naturally controlled by antioxidants.
Antioxidants are molecules that are capable of preventing free radicals from causing damage to healthy, fully functioning cells. When there's a deficiency of antioxidants, damage caused by free radicals can become debilitating and increasing.

What About Those Antioxidants?

Antioxidants are able to stabilize or deactivate free radicals before they attack the cells of your body. The antioxidants are able to break the chain reaction caused by free radicals by giving up an electron to the unstable molecules. Although your body creates some antioxidants naturally, these life-protecting nutrients are commonly found in fruits and vegetables. While there are thousands of antioxidants of different kinds found in nature, two of the most effective are the polyphenols and the flavanoids.

Antioxidants tend to work in one of two ways. When a free radical releases or takes an electron, a second radical is formed. This molecule then does the same thing to a third molecule, continuing to create unstable free radicals again and again. This process continues on and on until either the radical neutralized by a chain-breaking antioxidant like beta-carotene, vitamin C, or vitamin E, or it simply decays until it becomes a harmless product.

The second way that they work is preventive. Antioxidant enzymes prevent oxidation by slowing the rate of chain initiation. In other words, they hunt down the initiating radicals and prevent an oxidation chain from ever beginning its cycle. These antioxidants can also prevent oxidation by stabilizing metal radicals, such as copper and iron.

There are a few nutrients in food that contain antioxidants. Adding more fruit and vegetables in general to your diet will help to improve your health, but some foods are higher in antioxidants than others. The three major antioxidant vitamins are beta-carotene, vitamin C, and vitamin E. You can find them in colorful fruits and vegetables, especially those that are purple, blue, red, orange, and yellow. Vitamins C and E and beta-carotene are some of the most commonly studied antioxidants that are considered a dietary requirement.

Ann's reports on behalf of their mother-in-law, who suffered so greatly because of sciatic nerve damage that she was unable to leave her house for ten years unless she was transported in the back of a van while lying on a mattress because the pain was so unbearable. In the past two weeks, after drinking just two bottles of Monavie, she has been scrubbing her bathroom floor on her hands and knees and spent the day with her grandson at the beach picking up seashells for a five-hour trip to the beach, ending the day without any pain and still full of energy. She attributes her miracle recovery to Monavie.

Vitamin C is probably the most well-known of all the antioxidants. It is also the most important water-soluble antioxidant in extracellular fluids because it helps to neutralize reactive oxygen species (ROS) in the water or liquid phase before it can attack the lipids. Another benefit of vitamin C is that it is capable of regenerating vitamin E. Vitamin E is the most important lipid-soluble antioxidant. It is important because it is the chain-breaking antioxidant inside the cell membrane. It can protect the fatty acids.

Polyphenols are the natural chemicals that are responsible for the color, flavor, and scent in fruits and vegetables. Berries that are deeply pigmented, such as the acai berry, are especially high in these antioxidants. Polyphenols are often found in the outer layer of fruits and offer protection from harmful bacteria and UV light. In humans, polyphenols support cardiovascular health and protect your body from the damage called by oxidative stress.

Research on the various effects of polyphenols on human health has developed quite a bit in the past ten years. It strongly supports the idea that polyphenols play a role in the prevention of cardiovascular diseases and cancers. The antioxidant properties that polyphenols offer have been widely studied. Polyphenols are normally the most abundant antioxidants found in the common diet. They are most commonly consumed as fruits or plant-based drinks, such as fruit juice, tea, coffee, and red wines.

Current research-based evidence strongly suggests that polyphenols contribute to the prevention of cancers, cardiovascular conditions, and even osteoporosis. It also suggests that polyphenols play a role in the prevention of diabetes and degenerative brain diseases.

The MonaVie juice blends contain nutrients that work to help your body battle against aging and various other symptoms that are associated with oxidative stress. In fact, four ounces of their juice can provide you with the antioxidant capacity of up to 13 servings of common fruits and vegetables.

MonaVie Products

Ranging from powerful support with antioxidants to heart, joint, and immune health, MonaVie products are specially designed to provide the nutrition that your body needs to maintain the healthy and active lifestyle that you enjoy. They deliver a wide variety of products with beneficial ingredients such as Wellmune, plant-based glucosamine, and plant sterols. Every serving of their drinks is as healthy as it is delicious.

Every one of the MonaVie health-conscious products features a unique blend of the Brazilian acai berry, one of nature's most valued superfoods as well as 18 other fruits that are beneficial to your health, including cupacu, camu, blueberry, bilberry, acerola, pomegranate, and aronia, among a great deal of other beneficial fruits and vegetables.

With its blend of 19 fruits, including the famed acai, MonaVie health juice blends are fully packed with the nutrition that you need to feel and perform at your best every day. The acai berry has always been the foundation of the MonaVie juice blends, but they don't want to focus on only one while there are quite literally thousands of other phytonutrients and antioxidants found in nature's fresh fruits. This led to MonaVie selecting the 18 other fruits that they included in the juice blends. Each of the chosen fruits was selected for its unique and beneficial properties in addition to its ability to contribute to the variety of phytonutrients and antioxidants found in their premier nutritional drinks. All these fruits work together to provide an effect far beyond the reaches of what any single fruit could ever hope to do.

MonaVie offers a full line of health juice blends that promote overall health and well-being in individuals. MonaVie MX is a three-in-one juice blend that provides a great deal of support from antioxidants while also promoting joint health and the body's immune system. Filled with fruity flavonoids, this wellness drink offers a wider array of antioxidants than their other regular blend by blending together 19 fruits and 11 vegetables. The formula for this drink features BioEssence for increased bioavailability as well as their patented AcaVie, which is the purest and most potent form of the acai berry available. This juggernaut of a juice blend also includes glucosamine to help increase joint mobility and flexibility in addition to Wellmune, which has been clinically proven to strengthen the immune system. Maximize your health with MonaVie MX.

Miguel suffers from pain and inflammation in the sides of his eyes, but after drinking a single bottle of Monavie his problems are gone. He no longer needs to take a prescription medication he was on and no longer needs to use his eye glasses, because Monavie has fixed his eye troubles.

If you're looking for a drink that will get your body all of the essentials that it needs, then look no further than MonaVie's juice blend Essential. MonaVie Essential has been scientifically formulated to support the nutritional needs of the human body. MonaVie Essential is an effective blend that works to help your body defend against the effects of aging while aiding its overall health at the same time. This healthy juice blend is completely fortified with various super-fruits, fiber, and vitamins A, C, and E and features a mix of fruits that will benefit your body by nourishing it with powerful antioxidants and nutrients. Drink MonaVie Essential and put antioxidants for you today.

Get your move on with MonaVie Active. MonaVie Active is a delicious blend of 19 fruits that work to improve your body and is fortifies with powerful superfruits, fiber, and vitamins A, C, and E. This healthy blend will target joint mobility and flexibility. It will also work to promote your body's overall health and wellness. During a 12-week-long study involving MonaVie Active, all of the participants showed a significant improvement in their range of motion of their lumbar region and knees. Additionally, the participants noted a significant decrease in general discomfort around weeks 8 and 12. This was no doubt due to MonaVie Active's unique blend of pear, pomegranate, prunes, jabuticaba, maqui, kiwi, cranberry, grape, cupuacu, camu, black currants, blueberry, bilberry, aronia, apple, banana, and acerola with their proprietary blend of carotenoids, glucosamine, and their patented Acavie, which contains the most concentrated form of the berry available on the market.

Never worry about your heart's health again when you try MonaVie Pulse. With a blend of fruits chosen especially for their ability to support cardiovascular health nutritionally, MonaVie Pulse gives your body the antioxidants that it needs to keep your heart healthy. Studies have suggested that plant sterols play a key role in lowering cholesterol, so they have added them into this blend to help you keep your body balanced. With the addition of plant sterols and resveratrol, keeping your cholesterol levels in check has never been easier. Cardiovascular disease has long been a major concern in the United States and has become the leading cause of death across the nation. Keeping your heart healthy has never been more important. Discover the beat of a healthy heart with MonaVie Pulse.

If you have ever been concerned with your body's defenses, safeguard yourself with MonaVie (M)mun. MonaVie (M)mun works to arm your body against the common challenges that you face every day. A special blend of 19 fruits and Wellmune, a beta-glucon that has been clinically proven to fortify your body's immune system, allows this advanced juice blend to fight cellular oxidation and bolster your body's defenses all year round. With special inclusions like baobab, blood orange, elderberry, lingonberry, seabuckthorn, and

Wellmune, let MonaVie (M)mun be the bodyguard for your body and safeguard it against potentially harmful microorganisms while fighting oxidative damage and any signs of aging.

For those of you who are trying to keep kosher, MonaVie has you covered. MonaVie Kosher incorporates an approach to nutrition that follows the rules of balance, moderation, and variety. MonaVie Kosher is a delicious fusion of the acai berry of Brazil and 18 other fruits that will benefit your body in a number of different ways. MonaVie Kosher adheres to all kosher dietary laws and has been certified by the Orthodox Union of North America as well as the Chief Rabbinate of Israel. MonaVie Kosher still features a wide array of nutrients that will allow you to optimize your health while delivering the antioxidant capacity of 12 to 14 servings of fruits and vegetables in just four ounces. If you wish to see the official certificate from the Orthodox Union of North America, you can visit the MonaVie Kosher page of the company website.

Get Energized

MonaVie's line of energy drinks contain formulas that feature Palatinose, an energy source found naturally in carbohydrates in honey, sugar beets, and sugar cane that are fortified with completely natural sources of energy. Palatinose metabolizes more slowly than the ingredients found in typical energy drinks, and this promotes a steady stream of energy that lasts over a longer period of time.

MonaVie E and E Lite were ranked number one over the leading energy drinks in independent taste tests and were preferred for their color, sweetness, and aftertaste. A separate marketing analysis of 30 different energy drinks in both the retail and direct sales channels, which included the top five selling products, showed that 97 percent of the drinks contain artificial colors, sweeteners, flavors, and/or preservatives. Why take in all those artificial substances when you can have an energy drink that is completely natural and delicious? MonaVie E and MonaVie E Lite contain a blend of antioxidant rich fruits, including the superfoods acai and cupuacu. Both drinks are made with the naturally invigorating and delicious taste of fruit juice, which provides the energy enhancing nutrients within its refreshing taste.

MonaVie E and MonaVie E Lite promise one hundred percent natural energy without the side effects of jittering or crashing. When you drink MonaVie E or MonaVie E Lite, all you're getting is pure, natural energy. Without synthetic stimulants, the advanced formulas used to make these drinks provide a healthy alternative to the other energy drinks on the market. The one hundred percent natural energy blends contain ingredients that provide the quick pick me up and long, lasting energy that you need to be at your best. Use MonaVie E and MonaVie E Lite to get the energy you need when you need it without having to worry about any unwelcome side effects.

These drinks are specially designed with Palatinose to provide energy that lasts longer without the highs and lows that are associated with typical energy drinks. They also feature all natural, healthy sources of energy that promise to increase vigor, performance, alertness, and endurance when you need it.

Need an extra boost of energy but are worried about the calories? MonaVie E Lite only contains 90 calories per can because it is sweetened with the calorie free stevia, which is the most pure stevia leaf extract on the market.

RVLutionize Your Weight Loss

Looking to lose some weight? Regardless of whether you want to lose a little weight or a lot of weight, maintain your current weight, or improve your overall nutrition and well-being, MonaVie RVL is the weight solution that you need to help you on your way. MonaVie RVL is made to ensure that each calorie is as packed with nutrition as possible to make sure that you are working at the core of weight management.

The most important factor in weight management is nutrition. You can exercise as much as you want, but without the proper nutrition, you might actually do damage to your body. Ensuring that you get the nutrients that your body needs allows it to function properly, and that is the first step when it comes to weight management. The MonaVie RVL product line helps you manage your weight in a healthy way. Every snack you get is filled with a diverse amount of food and nutrients that will keep you focused on your goals while maintaining your health.

This product isn't just for people who have always struggled with health problems; Jennifer from Ontario developed gestational diabetes only recently, due to her pregnancy. Drinking Monavie for only five days, she has been able to stop taking her insulin because this juice keeps her blood sugar under control, even when she gives in to cravings for chocolate or cookies. She articulates that this is a wonderful product and is amazed at how quickly it was able to help her.

The MonaVie RVL's delicious shakes, snacks, and protein bars will satisfy your craving and give you the confidence you need to know that your body is in the right hands. MonaVie RVL also features a supplement that is designed to boost your metabolism. The Mona-Vie RVL line has everything you need in a weight management solution and will work to give you everything needed for you to reach your ideal weight.

Why are so many people raving about MonaVie RVL? Well, start using the products today and watch those unwanted pounds melt away. Try MonaVie RVL and be the you that you want to be without having to starve yourself or kill yourself at the gym. Who said weight management had to be a hassle? This is another reason distributers have such success with prospects. Because prospects see and feel the difference after using MonaVie products.

Whether you're looking to lose weight or simply control and maintain it, MonaVie RVLution can help you reach and keep your goal. MonaVie's own nutrition and fitness expert, Mark Macdonald, is the author of the New York Times bestselling book "Body Confidence." Mark Macdonald knows what it takes to manage weight, and he can help you no matter what your goal may be. Mark Macdonald has helped thousands of people burn fat, build muscle, and increase their energy with an approach to weight management that doesn't involve only eating healthily; it involves eating correctly.

When you join the MonaVie 90-day RVLution Program with Mark Macdonald, you'll receive the Ultimate Workout Series. The Ultimate Workout Series includes eight highly specialized workouts that will exercise your entire body. All of these workouts were special-ly designed to work with the MonaVie RVLution Program. With no complicated equipment involved, you'll be able to complete the series no matter where you go or when you need to work out.

As a member of the MonaVie 90-day RVLution program, you'll also receive the RVLution Booklet. This booklet will provide the crucial information that you will need to take control of your health and gain real body confidence while looking and feeling your best. The RVLution booklet will lead your through the 90-day program and provide you with all the solutions that you need. With the booklet, you'll be able to learn about the power of stabilizing your blood sugar and why most dieting fails, find the importance of MonaVie RVL and the three phases of the program, learn how to start, set your goals, and build your foundation, and establish a plan for exercising, sleeping, and managing stress.

As you experience success with the MonaVie 90-day RVLution program, you will have all the tools to break through any plateaus and RVL a lifestyle, not just a diet.

When you join the MonaVie 90-day RVLution program, you will also gain access to RVLution Online. In the online program, you'll have full access to their team of nutrition experts for support as well as the Delicious Recipe Database, which has thousands of meal options. Their team of experts will also help you develop customized meal plans that are specific to your needs and preferences in addition to a personalized exercise plan that will ensure faster results than any ordinary workout program. There will also be an interactive goal charts, a jump start phase that will promote your metabolism, and weekly coaching webinars that are led by Mark Macdonald himself.

No matter what your goal may be, RVL has something that can benefit you. Whether you are a part of the MonaVie 90-day RVLution program or working on your own plan for weight management, MonaVie's special line of RVL products can help you reach your goal. Everyone knows that every calorie counts when it comes to managing and losing weight. However, many people might be unaware that there are smart calories. That is what you'll find in MonaVie RVL Nutrition Shake Mix. These calories are nutrient dense and provide a high return on your intake so that you can stock up on nutrients while keeping your calorie count low. The MonaVie RVL Nutrition Shake Mix contains and delivers a broader array of nutrients to your body than a typical meal does, and it does it with half the calories.

MonaVie RVL Nutrition Shake Mix features AcaVie, which is the purest and most potent form of the acai berry that is available today, so each serving of the mix will help you manage your weight in a healthy and nutritious way. Nutrition has never tasted as good as it has with MonaVie RVL Nutrition Shake Mix. You choose how to prepare your shake. Simply replace the meal of your choice with the MonaVie RVL Nutrition Shake Mix by combining one scoop of the powder with 8 ounces of water or milk. To change things up or add an extra boost of nutrients, you can also add two ounces of one of your favorite MonaVie health juice blends. MonaVie RVL Nutrition Shake Mix is the most nutritious weight management solution available, and it works to help you maintain your lean muscle mass while fighting hunger so that you consume fewer calories throughout the day.

John has type two diabetes. John emphasizes that he sells the product because he believes in it--it does work. It has controlled his blood sugar and has totally relieved his back pains.

Another feature of the MonaVie RVL product line is the Mona-Vie RVL HDH Pro 10 Protein Bar. The MonaVie RVL HDH Pro 10 Protein Bar has been designed to allow for maximum protein absorption and features the concentrated antioxidant power of the acai berry and high-DH hydrolyzed whey protein, which is one of the most advanced quickest absorbing proteins out on the market today. The MonaVie RVL HDH Pro 10 Protein Bar helps to promote fat burning, weight management, body repair, and the building of lean muscle mass, all while fueling your body and controlling your appetite. The MonaVie RVL HDH Pro 10 Protein Bar is great for use prior to any workout session or any time that you want to satisfy your hunger.

The MonaVie RVL HDH Pro 10 Protein Bar is a great snack to use for any time of the day, and it tastes so good that you'll start to crave it instead of any other foods.

The MonaVie RVL product line also includes the MonaVie RVL Dietary Supplement. Even though regular exercise and eating a sensible, healthy diet are key to any proper weight management plan, sometimes running or swimming laps and counting all your calories just are not enough. Now, you will be able to boost your metabolism naturally with the MonaVie RVL Dietary Supplement. This dietary supplement boasts a powerful blend of antioxidants from eight different vegetables in each capsule. The all natural formula also includes AcaVie, their patented concentrated form of acai that is the most potent available on the market, and green tea that has been validated by clinical research. The MonaVie RVL Dietary Supplement helps your body to naturally burn more calories and aids in the reduction of body fat while providing a powerful blend of antioxidants that will promote your overall health.

Can't Sleep? Reset With Vset

MonaVie Vset is a powerful supplement that helps to reduce stress, anxiety, and fatigue in your body by rebalancing stress hormones. MonaVie Vset is designed to help you relax and revitalize to give you a good night's sleep and higher levels of physical and mental energy throughout the day. The proprietary formula used in this supplement will work to improve your overall well-being while balancing your biochemistry so that you do not burn out in the middle of the day. Try MonaVie Vset and never worry about resting again.

Bottom Line: With their different product lines, they at MonaVie are here to ensure that their customers get the best product available to them. Beyond great taste, they want everyone who tries their products to feel healthier and fitter. Whether you choose to go all out with the MonaVie 90-day RVLution program or simply want to enjoy one of their healthy juice blends to promote wellness in your body, they at MonaVie work to make sure that you're getting a quality product.

Having these great products allows the modern day entrepreneur to focus on their core activity, building their marketing business. This leads us to the next part of the book, business building.

Betty, from Florida, has struggled with high cholesterol. She excitedly claims that her cholesterol dropped from 197 to 161 after drinking Monavie for only three weeks. She continues that though she has suffered from leg pain due to poor circulation for years, since beginning this method of treatment her legs feel great. She states, "I truly believe in this product."

Modern Marketing

A little over a decade ago, social media and online social networks did not really exist. However, practically every single large company in addition to many small businesses put their resources into building their presence online. Many of them have created corporate accounts on certain social media sites, and they spend their time and money interacting with as many users as possible, boosting their fan base, posting and broadcasting meaningful content, monitoring the comments left by users inside and outside of their page or group, and measuring the results of their various marketing campaigns.

Over the last decade, social media has grown to the point where it simply cannot be ignored by any company, large or small, because they would miss out on far too many opportunities and fade into the unknown. After all, Facebook alone has hundreds of millions, if not yet a billion, of active users, and their average user has over a hundred friends. Twitter, too, has hundreds of millions of users that generate about half a million tweets a day. YouTube receives billions of views daily. LinkedIn has over a hundred million registered users. The amount of people actively using these sites are simply too high and too diverse to ignore.

Social media took the business world by storm, and the direct selling segment of the market has been no exception. The thing that started as a technological trend has become a central, core aspect of how direct sales companies do business today, and they at MonaVie are no different. They would also like to encourage their distributers to take advantage of this as well.

During my research for this book, I came across a very successful, but retired networker named Dave. He's not part of MonaVie, but was hired to do some private coaching for one key MonaVie team. He coached telephone recruiting. One interesting point he made was the case for sounding strong on the phone and keeping control. This he said was one of the biggest challenges people had.

He showed me a small paper file that he called his secret weapon that eliminated this problem, and told me he was planning on giving it away on Amazon for 99 cents as a Kindle book. He laughingly said it was a little book of only 130 lines or sentences that he has used and reused for years, with many different networking companies, but it was worth a million dollars! Because it's so small, few people would understand and value this tool, he added.

He said you could just pick a line at random if you were on the phone losing control to a prospect. After using a few lines of these lines, or statements, you would be back in control. It was perfect for prospecting calls and follow up calls.

I challenged him to release this information, and just before publication of this book, he let me know it was available as a Kindle book as of March, 18th.

It's not a big book, but it has great value. Here is the link, (it's not an affiliate link, just a direct link to Amazon). I think you'll find that for 99 cents you'll get the best value ever!

US Amazon http://www.amazon.com/Simplest-Shortest-Powerful-Marketing-ebook/dp/B00BW7KJ38

Canadian Amazon http://www.amazon.ca/Simplest-Shortest-Powerful-Marketing-ebook/dp/B00BW7KJ38

UK Amazon http://www.amazon.co.uk/Simplest-Shortest-Powerful-Marketing-ebook/dp/B00BW7KJ38

Or search Amazon for: The Simplest, Shortest, Most Powerful MLM and Network Marketing Prospect Control and Closing Lines and Scripts by David Williams.

The Benefits

Having an active presence on social media offers a number of benefits to companies of any size, shape, and industry. The most active social media sites can drive a great deal more traffic towards a company's website, promote the sale of the company's products, support recognition of and loyalty to the company's brand, and provide a link for direct communication to distributers and customers. Social media gives a brand the wonderful opportunity to express its personality. When dealing with direct sales, that can't be understated. The most obvious of the benefits that can come from having an active presence on social media sites is that companies can gain insights and feedback from the amount of communication that takes place there.

The main benefit of maintaining an active presence on social media sites is that you can hear directly and immediately from the consumers. Social media provides a method of two way communication. Building your community on social media takes, time, effort, resources, and people who are dedicated to the initiative. The feedback that you can get from people is such that you might get from a focus group, at a greatly reduced cost. Another benefit of working on social media sites is that they are driving up the search engine visibility of the companies that use them. Social media benefits the search engine optimization, and companies can do a lot to make sure that they have great content that aids in this.

Even though joining a social media site is usually free, the pure popularity of the social networking sites requires that companies devote significant levels of their resources to social media. There are many companies that employ full-time social media writers, directors, and so on whose jobs are dedicated to engaging with customers both prospective and current as well as distributers on sites, writing and broadcasting useful and thoughtful content, monitoring the comments 24 hours a day, and analyzing the results of everything that goes on in the site.

An anonymous person from North Charleston, SC reports in that they do not buy nor sell Monavie, but they have a friend who drinks the product for her seizures. This friend was suffering from grand mal seizures weekly, but since beginning Monavie as a mode of treatment in August of 2007 she has only had one seizure, with this product to thank. Monavie has made a tremendous difference in her life.

Monitoring tools and content aggregators provide helpful assistance, but they come at a price. The greater toll here is the time that it takes to stay on top of all the posts and comments that come through social media. The investment that you make in working with social media is not so much a monetary investment as it is an investment of time, which ultimately means resources. Producing content that is thoughtful and meaningful in addition to monitoring social media sites takes a great deal of time. If the content that you are posting is not relevant, interesting, timely, and valuable, people will not continue to visit your site or will begin to ignore or block your posts. You also have to devote a lot of time to monitoring the sites, being sure that you are responsive to any and every comment or question that might be posted.

To truly be involved in social media means that MonaVie has had to become an organization that can quickly generate high quality word of mouth content. Luckily, as a community commerce company, they are quite familiar with producing this kind of content. This is rare among network marketing companies, who rely on distributers to do all the heavy lifting.

One other challenge of social media is that participation in these sites often makes it necessary to give up a certain level of control. They have no control over what their customers or competitors are going to post online, so they have to be prepared for how were are going to deal with posts that show up on your blog or Facebook wall that might be negative. Unfortunately, that is just one of the minuses of working with social media: there is no way to control what other people are posting about you, MonaVie, or their products. People can post positive comments, but they can also post negative ones and complaints. They have to be on their toes so that they can respond to these posts appropriately.

One way to handle negative comments is just to leave them alone. There are people out there who just do not like the direct selling industry, or they may have had a bad experience, so they post negative comments or stories online. As posts become commented on or are ranked, it draws relevance to that story, which will drive it up in search engine results. They certainly don't want that to happen, so if people have something bad to say, let them say it. If there's a negative comment that seems as though it is something that can be fixed, then that is the time to act.   Most of the time it's just a poorly trained member of a competing network marketing company, and not a real post.

Social media has changed how companies have to do business today. In the old days, if there was a customer who had a bad experience with customer service, there was no way for them really to tell people about it. Now, every company that does direct sales is on notice that they are just one unhappy customer away from a significant backlash against their brand. Even at MonaVie, they have experienced their fair share of this, but luckily they have had the proper leadership to wash off any grime that upset customers have thrown their way and climb back to the top.

Top companies such as Apple and Amazon are doing an exceptional job in terms of customer service. If they do not compare favorably with them, then their customers will send their money to them instead. Direct sales can no longer stay in living rooms or Holiday Inn conference rooms. After the rise of social media, they are now forced to go head to head with the Apples and Amazons of the world to win customer loyalty and spending.

Social Media Innovation

There have been some great innovations in the world of social media that have been made by businesses not too different from MonaVie. It's always important to try new things. If it works, you can share it with the other distributers at MonaVie, and who knows, it might even lead to your recommendation becoming a common sales tactic.

One example of innovation started in the past few is years is companies hosting Facebook chats, where experts from the company and customers can interact with the company via chat or on the company's Facebook wall. Depending on the skills of your experts, you might even be able to host a bilingual chat.

Another innovation to consider is hosting blogger events. If you are able to invite local bloggers to a special event, you can build a relationship with those bloggers in addition to meeting their fan base. These events will enable MonaVie and its distributers to build key relationships within their online community while also informing new members of the audience about their company and their products.

Some companies have mobile applications for smartphones that allow distributers to share the business and product opportunities. Applications like these are designed to act as full service applications that allow people to shop, share presentations, track volumes of shipments, and much, much more. It also allows them to view videos about the company and its products.

Do you have a great idea for a new way to use social media to the advantage of yourself and MonaVie? Go ahead and try it out! If it works out, share it with other distributers so that they can see how well it works with their audiences. After all, all of us at MonaVie is working as a team to benefit not only themselves, but the entire world.

How Direct Sellers Use Social Media

There are many different ways that direct selling companies use social media sites to their advantage. There is a great deal that they can all learn from each other, so it is a great idea to look to them for ideas of how they and their distributers can use it, too. Many of them use sites such as Twitter and Facebook of course, but others are also active on blogs, Foursquare, YouTube, and many other sites.

For some companies, social media networks are seen as a means of increasing engagement with both distributers and customers in addition to building the brand, marketing, and fostering public relations. Some companies use social media to work directly with only their distributers and existing customers because they view it as an engagement and management tool while others use it to attract new customers or introduce and test new products.

Social media is a fairly new channel for marketing, but there is a pretty strong consensus people share that it can aid in the growth of a business. Customers who interact with certain brands through some form of social media tend to spend 20 to 40 percent more money with those companies than other customers do. In addition to this, customers who engage with companies via social media generally show a stronger loyalty to the brands that they interact with.

Stew has Lupus Nephritis and has been on Monavie Active for nearly two years. He began taking this medicinal supplement following a bad flare-up that began to attack his kidneys. Chemo treatments hadn't didn't work for him and he was losing hope when his family practitioner recommend he start taking Monavie. Stew signed up to be a distributor but, concerned with selling a product that may not work, he only sold the product to himself. He explains tentatively that recovery is not a simple process that happens overnight; it takes one to two months before you may reap any benefits from Monavie. The product must get into your blood stream before the medicinal benefits can take effect. Stew trusted this medication because the doctor who recommended it had a son with cancer, and he went into remission with the aid of this juice and other holistic treatments. Stew explains that this isn't another pyramid scheme or a scam; this juice is high in antioxidants and vitamins the body needs but doesn't get on a daily basis. That is why it works.

The thing that few people realize with this, though, is that you can use social media to drive your direct sales, assuming that you have the proper strategy in place.

To attract and retain customers, you can use social broadcasting. Some people get the wrong idea about this when they hear the word "broadcasting." They assume that it is an old-school marketing technique that is used by "interruptive" marketers. The reality is that customers want to hear valuable information. They crave it. Developing your presence on social media, starting conversations with a suitably frequent amount of posts, or broadcasts in this case, and sharing the useful and valuable information that you are producing in your content will allow you to make the most of the direct sales opportunities that are available to you thanks to social media.

Social broadcasting can earn you the trust and attention of current and new customers alike, and this will ensure that anyone who is already buying from you will continue to do so and that anyone who doesn't buy from you will consider becoming one of your patrons. This strategy also gives you the chance to upsell and cross-sell, preferably in a tasteful manner, to the audience provided by your social media presence by highlighting the latest offers that you have and discussing the other products and services that you and their company offer.

This process usually starts with benchmarking. Depending on your current situation, this step may very well be a short one, particularly if you have little or no presence on social media at the moment. This will be your starting point and will help you create specific objectives for what you want to do with your social media presence, but be sure that you match them up with the internal business goals that you have already put in place.

For example, if you want to attract more women to your products or as recruits to your team, you should target your social media efforts with those women in mind. This might sound incredibly obvious, but keeping a conscious awareness of the objective will help you make smarter decisions further down the line in terms of what kind of broadcasts you make, what time you post them online, how you word and phrase your content, and so forth. It's important to set specific milestones for your broadcasts efforts on social media, but remember that you need to keep them flexible. This will allow for positive changes during the implementation of your broadcasts. Remember, you are dealing with people when you broadcast socially, so projections are not very likely to be completely accurate.

Selecting specific networks of social media and establishing your presence on those networks is crucial, of course, and the networks that you choose will depend heavily on your target audience. This basically means that you need to know where members of your target demographic are having conversations online, and you will need to make sure that you are there, too.

A very basic example of that idea is that Facebook is more appropriate for business to consumer marketers and that LinkedIn or similar sites are more appropriate for business to business marketers. There are obviously more specific details that must be considered, but the main point is that social media is constantly changing and new sites and networks are being introduced quite often, so it is important to focus on quality instead of quantity. In short, you want to produce great content that will engage your audience on a few platforms instead of boring or poorly written content on a lot of them. By focusing your time, money, and efforts on a few specific networks, you will more often than not receive far superior results than when you spread your resources thin by trying to be everywhere at the same time.

Once you have your sites chosen, you will have to balance your strategy for social media to find the right mixture of broadcast and interaction. Each of the two has its advantages, but you should use them together as part of a comprehensive approach to social media that will give you the best of the both of them. The best way to keep them balanced is to keep your customer's wants and needs at the forefront of your mind at all times.

Automate your broadcasts as a strategy used to target users who might be online outside of the hours that you usually interact on your social media. The automation of social media can also help to maintain consistency, which will enable you to set posts to go live and relax to some extent.

Obviously, a brand that does no posting on social media will quickly become an outcast. This is because networks such as Facebook are meant to be hubs for conversations. In a similar sense, even though Twitter is more often used as a stream of posts, businesses that take their Twitter followers for granted and only tweet bulk automated posts frequently throughout the day will find that they are losing the attention of their followers quite quickly.

Jeff has been overweight for most of his life, struggling to lose weight without much result. Between January to September of 2011, on Monavie Active, he has lost 310 lbs. and is proud to say he is now around 255 lbs. He is happy to finally have found a great product that has worked for him, after so many other products did not.

Another good idea is to create some basic guidelines for your-self or your staff to follow when using social media. That will help to keep you and everyone involved focused and aware of their bounda-ries, and this will allow you to avoid issues such as the duplication of messages or content that doesn't reflect the voice you want finding its way into your social channels. Focus and monitor how your broad-casts are doing, and pay close attention to the impact that they have on actual sales. An example of something that you might want to try to broadcast could be tweeting a link to a MonaVie blog post that shows how their products help people maintain their overall health.

Another technique that their distributers might want to try is social listening. There is a great deal of data that is related to pur-chasing being shared every day across all of the main social media platforms. With a presence on social media, you will be able to monitor and capitalize on those opportunities.

You might be answering questions, helping customers solve problems by suggesting solutions, waving away potential concerns that people might have, or merely sharing a link to a blog post that will offer more information on a specific topic that a prospective client has expressed an interest in. There is an abundance of tools that you can use for social listening and monitoring that is available to help you drive sales via social media. They all have benefits and draw-backs, so which one you use will ultimately come down to how much money you're willing to spend, what you want to do with them, and how comfortable you are with using these tools. Should you decide to use one of these tools, you'll be spending a lot of time becoming familiar with that tool's dashboard, so you will want to be sure that you are able to get the most out of it.

As one of their distributers, there are a few key areas that you'll want to focus on. You will want to look for mentions of the MonaVie brand, both positive and negative, and try to enhance the person who left the comment's interaction with their brand.

Direct sales over social media does not always, not does it have to, mean immediate sales. You can also try to identify who the key influencers in a niche or market segment are and develop a relationship with them. These people are more likely to have clout with hundred or maybe even thousands of potential customers. Think about how beneficial it could be to deliver excellent customer service to and build a relationship with a blogger who might in turn write a post about how great MonaVie and their products are!

Combining trigger phrases with topic area monitoring is a good way to develop prospective clients who perhaps recognize that they have something that they need or want but are not quite sure what the solution is yet. If you listen for these people and help to guide them toward MonaVie by feeding them content that is useful, over a slightly longer timeline, you will be generating sales for your MonaVie products.

One very common and very useful application of your presence on social media will be listening and responding to any questions that your customers might have about MonaVie or their products. Even though this is quite common, it should never be forgotten about. Everyone at MonaVie and around the world knows the importance of resolving customer problems and complaints that have been voiced over some social network. The important thing to remember here is that they all need to remain aware of customer complaints so that they can take care of them before that complaint spreads or goes viral. Another great thing about customer questions is that there are often sales opportunities in them. If it seems tasteful, be ready to respond to a customer's question with an up-sell or a cross-sell.

How to command a terrific social media presence without spending any time on it

If the whole concept of building a social media presence, blogging, reacting, and building social media pages scares you, or you feel it will take too much of your time, borrow a secret from the pros: outsource to a social media pro.

Outsourcing: The short cut to wealth

Outsourcing is the contracting out of an internal business process to a third party. The practice of contracting a business process out to a third party rather than staffing it internally (or doing it yourself) is common in the modern economy. The term "outsourcing" became popular in the United States near the turn of the 21st century. (Wikipedia).

Danay has lupus. She was on a number of various medications, none of which were doing her much good. She began drinking Monavie in February of 2008 and, since then, she is off all her medications and reports that she is feeling wonderful. Her doctor encourages her to continue drinking Monavie, recognizing how significantly her health has improved, even without her meds. She reports that she has absolutely no pain, and endless amounts of energy. She exclaims, "This is a wonderful product."

What does this mean to you? If there are portions of building a social media presence that is overwhelming to you, you can find a social media pro that resides in a country overseas, where the wages are different. For example, many people in India, Pakistan, and the Philippines, to name only a few, are very social media savvy and read and write English as well as the average American. Yet for a small sum, sometimes just $5 to $10 per week, they will run your entire social media presence, post, follow up, re-tweet, seek useful information to pass on, and generally act like you. This will pay off big dividends in the long term, and can be started and created by your outsourcer while you are at home building your local business.

You can find social media administrators on sites like fiverr.com as well as other outsourcing sites like freelance.com, elance.com, etc. Spend a little time on fiverr.com to see all of the different jobs you can outsource. If you need a Facebook fan page made, don't waste time, just outsource it and get it done. Later, as you earn more, you can hire better and better freelancers and build up your brand, which brings up the next important section.

In the business world of today, and all over the internet, you will read about the importance of branding. From car manufactures to online shoe stores, from Disney World to American Airlines, branding is important. But you, as an independent distributer are not 'MonaVie'. You are your own brand. This is why you need to build yourself up in the world of social media as someone who is a 'go to person' for health, and as you succeed, for wealth.

If you see yourself as the brand, your task is easier. You can create YouTube videos that speak of a great way to lose weight, to get healthy, etc., as long as you don't use the MonaVie brand name. Encourage people to seek you out, so they come to YOU, asking YOU what you are offering.

Understanding that YOU are the brand, and not MonaVie, is a major concept for success in network marketing.

Consider this – someone asks you 'what do you do?'

Answer 1 'I'm in MonaVie'

Answer 2 'I recently established a company that is seeking distribution for a major but unknown Brazilian natural remedy', (you are your own company). 'Who do you know in (blank – their area) that is entrepreneurial minded?'.

Do you get the point? You have far better control being the brand, being yourself, and not trying to be the corporation. Now, this is just an example, your upline team member can offer you all sorts of good opening lines and ice breakers to use when speaking to prospects, but this will get you started.

Real-Time Chances

There are always opportunities for you as a distributer to sell or even expand your business with MonaVie. When you're representing MonaVie online, try to remember that any business is much more likely to interact with key decision makers in a home or in a company if they respond to a question in less than an hour. Companies around the world have recognized the importance of this strategy, so as a fast growing community commerce company, they at MonaVie recognize the importance of this as well. Use their experience and the experiences of other companies to help you grow your own business. Real-time action via the proper social channel can provide you with the opportunity to increase your sales significantly.

If you have trained your outsourcer well, they can handle these for you. If they are new, have them alert you to this opportunity to help a potential prospect.

This message can be applied to social listening and general responses alike. If you are checking in or only taking advantage of these opportunities once a day, you will find that you are missing a great chance to make and increase your sales. When prospective customers ask a question about their products to their friends, they are more than likely willing to purchase. A friend could easily talk them over to one of their competitor's products or a rival brand might try to chime in on their discussion, and you will have missed an opportunity for what could have been a fairly easy sale.

Something to Consider

When you create a presence for yourself online related to MonaVie, you are entering a social area where some of the users might not be aware that their posts or updates are accessible to the public whether it's by the use of social listening tools or you merely to happen upon them. Because of this and the fact that you are representing MonaVie and their products, it is important that you make the message appropriate for where that prospective customer might be in the decision making process. Jumping in and trying a hard sell when your prospective customer seems to be unready to buy might come off as a bit creepy. Enticing a customer with a coupon code might be more appropriate if that customer is openly discussing whether he wants to purchase their products or the products of one of their competitors. That is the sort of thoughtful and considerate message that is more likely to align with the state of mind of that particular customer or client, and it will almost definitely lead you to a sale.

All her life, Alma has suffered from Lupus, and just recently was diagnosed with Lymphoma as well. She suffered from night sweats, preventing her from getting any rest. Alma struggled to find some sort of medication or medicinal product to help her and not long ago discovered Monavie, which she believes has been her miracle cure. She is now able to sleep and has far more energy. She claims that she is now able to live "a healthier life." She highly recommends anyone with similar problems try Monavie, guaranteeing they will see improvement within a week of using this great product.

The Future of Social Media

So, what lies ahead for direct sales and social media? Some social media experts believe that companies need to keep their eyes on mobile technology and social search. Mobile technology is constantly changing and improving. New features are being added each time a phone is released, and people are spending less on computers and laptops because they use their phones and tablets as replacements. Social media will only become more and more integrated into mobile technology, so it is very important to stay at on top of what's going on with that industry while working to incorporate your MonaVie business into it. Much like social media of the past, it is simply a trend that cannot be ignored.

Another thing to consider is that social media sites can double as search engines. These days, when people want to find more information about something, many of them still use search engines such as Google or Bing, but more and more people are beginning to go directly to social media sites to learn about companies or products by accessing pages on their social network. This shouldn't be surprising because there is a large amount of trust among consumers who share space on the same social media sites. Almost everyone trusts recommendations from people who they already know, and a similar amount of people trust recommendations that come from people who they don't know personally, such as those in customer reviews or online posts. After friends and family, online reviews and feedback on social media sites are the number one driver for brand loyalty and recognition.

User-generated content is in a way the same as word of mouth advertising, just in an online format. When you look at it that way, there is no reason to wonder why customers trust it. Customers have relied on the networks that they trust, whether it was their friends, family, or neighbors, since long before Facebook was launched.

You have read a lot of MonaVie stories in this book. They all were researched by myself or my assistant before being added to this book MonaVie has had a lot of praise for its success in 'curing' a vast range of terrible illnesses. It should be made clear that Mona Vie, the company, makes no claims whatsoever about its product, as it is a food, and not a drug or similar product. Now, while the acai berry has been studied and is an amazing curative, for legal reasons, claims by food companies should not and cannot be made. This book was not written by anyone associated with MonaVie, and I, the author have no stake in the company's success.   It was only after careful research did I find overwhelming evidence of the curative properties of acai berry, the key ingredient in Movavie's product line. Clearly, after reading the peer reviewed material on acai berry, one can understand the amazing claims that individuals have made about Movavie's products. Having said that, this book is not to be taken as a replacement of medical advice from a professional and qualified medical person.

It must be remembered that MonaVie is a network marketing company and there are many people in OTHER network marketing companies that see any other company as a competitor. Many are jealous of Movavie's success and the ease that new distributers have in sharing their product. Enough people have something wrong with them that acai berry can help. They notice a positive reaction and either purchase the product and or outright join the business.   For this reason, MonaVie, the corporation, may find itself in hot water from authorities from time to time, reacting to a well prepared and organized barrage of complaints from frustrated competing network-ers. Some will just look for a reason to complain, while others will create letter writing campaigns to authorities suggesting that MonaVie is making 'medical claims'. This stems from some of it's over excited independent distributers 'telling their product success story'. No-where does MonaVie make claims about its products. In fact, it is a very good corporate citizen and attempts to keep its distributers in line with all of the rules and regulations.

Still, I felt it was important that I included some of the many, many voices of the people who are helped by consuming some of the many MonaVie products.

Tony's father was diagnosed with mesothelioma, a form of cancer caused by asbestos. Since being introduced to, and consuming the MonaVie Active, his Doctor now refers to him as the "miracle" patient who is (according to the tests) beating the cancer.

From Dr. Leonard Coldwell, as well known on late night radio as Dr. Oz is on early morning TV:

MonaVie is an all-natural health product that comes highly recommended by Dr. Hohn. MonaVie is a fruit drink made from a large variety of exotic fruits with the crown jewel being the acai berry, which is the main ingredient of the juice. The acai used in MonaVie is certified organic. Consuming only 2 ounces of juice twice daily will give you the approximate antioxidant capacity of 13 servings of fruits and vegetables. Below you will find more details about the company and its incredible products.

Product Overview

MonaVie's extraordinary products feature a delicious blend of the Brazilian acai berry and 18 other body-beneficial fruits from around the world. (acai, white grape, apple, acerola, aronia, purple grape, cranberry, passion fruit, prune, kiwi, blueberry, wolfberry, camu, pomegranate, lychee fruit, pear, banana, cupuaciu, and bilberry.)
MonaVie's refreshing acai blends are products with a purpose. From powerful antioxidant support to joint and heart health, each formula delivers key nutrients to help you maintain a healthy and active lifestyle.

Support your body's antioxidant and nutritional needs with MonaVie. Taking a Balance-Variety-Moderation approach to nutrition, this premier formula delivers powerful antioxidants and phytonutrients to help fight free radicals and maintain your body's overall health.

Enhance your body's joint health with MonaVie. This advanced formula features the added benefit of plant-derived glucosamine, which has been scientifically shown to promote healthy joint function by targeting mobility and flexibility. Designed to support joint performance and recovery, this vital formula delivers the resources your body needs to get moving.

Watching your cholesterol? MonaVie Pulse nutritionally supports your cardio-vascular system. With added heart health benefits derived from plant sterols* (which studies suggest play a key factor in lowering cholesterol) and resveratrol, maintaining healthy cholesterol levels has never been easier.

Recharge your body and mind with a boost of sustained energy. MonaVie features a proprietary blend of antioxidant rich fruits, including the Brazilian superfruit acai, and natural sources of energy. Great tasting and lightly carbonated, this healthy formula increases performance, endurance, and concentration by kicking up your energy level and keeping it there without a subsequent crash. Finally, a healthy solution to your body's everyday energy needs.

Delivers potent antioxidants and essential nutrients to your body. MonaVie Kosher is a mouthwatering fusion of the Brazilian acai berry one of nature's top superfoods and 18 other beneficial fruits. Incorporating a Balance-Variety-Moderation approach to nutrition, this free radical fighting, kosher certified formula nutritionally supports your body's overall health.

Optimize your body's natural defenses. MonaVie is a beneficial blend of 19 fruits and Wellmune® clinically shown to promote proper immune function. Formulated with antioxidant rich formula a proprietary complex featuring the superfruits acai and maqui, this delicious juice helps protect your body year round. It's your daily defense for a healthier life.

* Foods containing at least 0.4 grams per serving of plant sterols, eaten twice a day with meals for a daily total intake of at least 0.8 grams and as part of a diet low in saturated fat and cholesterol, may reduce the risk of heart disease. Two servings (4 ounces of juice or 2 packets of gel) of MonaVie Pulse contain 0.8 grams of plant sterols.

These statements have not been evaluated by the Food and Drug Administration. This product is not intended to diagnose, treat, cure, or prevent any disease.

Conclusion

Even after extensive research, I am always open to more views. If you have a MonaVie story to tell about how the product has changed your life or health, please send me your story. If you have a business success story, I welcome it too. My publisher will be updating both the Kindle and Paper versions of this book weekly, and your story can be in the book. Email me at Kevin_Lindsey@AllAmericanISP.com. By sending me your story, you give me the right to publish it. I may edit it for readability.

My research on MonaVie and those associated with it has made me truly appreciate the amazing opportunity that it provides. It is just in its infancy, here in April of 2013, and I predict it to become a major dominate contributor to health, wellness and prosperity for those who are smart enough to commit themselves to spreading the word of MonaVie and acai berry.

If you enjoyed this book, please leave an honest review on Amazon. Reviews help others find books that interest them, and help authors do a better job in their next book. If you enjoyed this book and have an interest in MonaVie, leaving a review here can help spread the word about your MonaVie story. If you have constructive suggestions, please write to me at the email above.

I wish each and every one of you a full and abundant life, jam-packed with health, adventure and financial security. Kevin

If you wish to order this book in bulk quantities please email my office for shipping rates at: Kevin_Lindsey@AllAmericanISP.com
10 or more - $4.00 each
25 or more - $3.50 each
50 or more - $3.15

Some "How to" books to explode your business:

How to Recruit Doctors into your MLM or Network Marketing team by showing them a NO Warm Market System

http://www.amazon.com/Recruit-Doctors-Network-Marketing-ebook/dp/B00CCPZ7Z4

Where to Find Doctors – It's not where you think

A new source of Doctors (medical) who are not busy

Perfect for the Wellness Industry

No buying Leads

Not working the phone

This book is going to teach you an amazing system to recruit Doctors and an amazing system for you to build a huge, profitable and unstoppable leg under them - without the Doctor using any of their warm market, 'buying leads' or touching the phone!

Full Discloser: This is a short book. It's less than 50 pages long. It contains no fluff or padding. It's direct and to the point. The system contained is worth hundreds of thousands of dollars in sales, and could retire you. Really. Forget the low price of $8.99, forget the number of pages. This book will show you a fool proof system that ANY one can follow to build an unstoppable MLM Network Marketing business by recruiting Doctors. I have made it newbie friendly, but those with experience will take this system and put into practice very quickly.

This book will cover, step by step, and in very detailed and specific language:

How to recruit Doctors

The 'invisible' secret source of Doctors without a practice that are begging for something like what you will be able to show them

How to recruit busy Doctors with a practice and zero time

How to avoid the 'I don't want to go to my contacts/warm market' objection because you will be teaching them a system that requires ZERO warm market

And No 'buying leads'!

How to fill, yes FILL, meeting rooms with prospects all eager to join and try your products

NO conference calls, webinars, websites, Fanpages, autoresponders etc.

This is the full system, from the free ads you will place to the words on the marketing material you will print. This approached is very inexpensive to follow, quick and easy to implement, and very straight forward.

Also included are the phone scripts and person to person scripts you need to use when speaking to the Doctors, their receptionists, and to use in getting the appointment.

Forget all the 'usual suspects' techniques, this is not about dropping off DVDs, inviting them to conference calls, or creating special 'Doctors only' presentations. Forget all of that, and forget all of your old scripts and ads.

This system works for Doctors and requires NO Warm Market – I know I said that above, but it's very important you know this.

You don't need any paid advertising, Facebook, Internet, Twitter etc., this is all offline, local, and affordable.

No one has taught you this before. Guaranteed.

I'm going to show you where to get Doctors and how to approach them. This book will reveal to you a hidden world of Doctors who are not busy. I am going to share with you this source, give you all the scripts, the ads, the marketing materials, right down to what to say in the low cost marketing material.

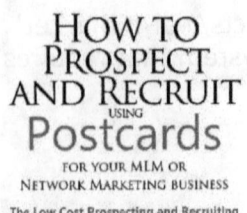

http://www.amazon.com/Postcards-Marketing-Prospecting-Recruiting-ebook/dp/B00EVZG8R4

Fed up not having quality leads?

Are you in a MLM company you love, but just can't find REAL prospects to talk to?

Tried 'online' leads but found you just wasted your time and money?

Many networkers are well past the 'warm market' stage, and are struggling to find success. It seems the entire world has gone online and the problem that networkers face is sticking out in an ever increasing ocean of websites, mobile apps, opt-in forms, blog posts, Facebook Likes, Youtube movies and Tweets. It never ends.

There is alternative. There is another way.

Because the world HAS gone online, good old fashioned Direct Mail is making a comeback. Why? Because no one gets 'real' mail anymore. You have zero competition!

And what's more real than a picture postcard?

NOTE:

What This Book is NOT about: this book in no way teaches you to send those ugly, tacky, pre-printed, glossy pictures of fast expensive cars or mansions, or YELLOW 'print your own' postcards. NO, NO, NO!

If you are engaged in postcard marketing, buying glossy tacky 'in your face' MLM style postcards and mailing them out – or worse – paying to have them mailed out – I'll show you a method that will increase your success by a massive amount – because I guarantee your message will be read if you use the method I teach.

Or, if you are prospecting with one of those 'print your own' cards at the local Office Max, mailing out thousands until you're broke by sending ugly cards – you will be so happy switching to my method because it will save you time, money, you'll mail out less cards and get massive more results.

Again, because I guarantee your prospect will read your message.

I will show you a method that combines two of the most important recruiting factors for success in MLM:

Mass Recruiting

and

Personalization

And NO – this is not about using computer 'hand writing fonts'!!!

No, I'll show you a method to recruit massively with postcards, in a very personalized way for your prospect to find it impossible to not read your message and make a call.

This works.   This book is based on my famous postcard seminars that were part of a $10,000 MLM insider's weekend training. You will get this same information for less than $10. And the best part of it is, this system works even better today than before! Why? Because the power of a postcard, personalized, is stronger today in this Internet age.

Full Disclosure: This is a short, to the point book. It's not full of padding or fluff, (however, I do trace for you how I discovered my introduction into Direct Mail for MLM Recruiting by a presidential fundraiser).

It's a 'How To' book. You are paying for the system, the magic, and the fact that you won't need any other information to get started.

I have included low or no budget methods as well.

Please NOTE: This book is for MLM or Network Marketing recruiting – it's not about postcard 'marketing' for non-MLM business. The information here is for network marketers who want to build downlines and offer a system to their team that does not rely on 'buying leads' from the internet and telemarketing 'survey leads', 'real time leads', 'fresh leads', or any of the other scammy descriptions of absolutely terrible leads for sale by lead companies.

Looking for a Low cost, but highly efficient network marketing tool way to get REAL leads? This is it.

Forget Internet leads – recruit real people, not virtual names.

How to Prospect and Recruit using Postcards for your MLM or Network Marketing Business - The Low cost Prospecting and Recruiting Tool that Out Performs Online Methods is a complete method. Includes the way to personalize the cards, where to buy them at the best prices, how to produce them, where to get the lists to mail your cards to, as well as how to do this on a low or no budget.

You will also get a '24 hour' message to load up on your voice mail system to take all the calls you'll get from your prospects.

How to create the personalized card

Where to get your cards wholesale

What to say on the card

Where to get lists and how to deal with list brokers

Low and no budget tricks and strategies

Text for your 24 hour message your prospects calls after reading your card

If you have run out of ways of recruiting, if your upline is no help, take action yourself and invest in your business by using this book on how to recruit and build a team with postcards.

This system works in USA, Canada and Europe – I know because I have used it in each of those countries and built huge downlines in this way.

Now, this book, I'll tell you upfront it's not for newbies. If you are not in the market for new scripts, you don't need this book. But if you are looking for more ideas and scripts for building your business, this is unlike any script book you have ever read. For those in MonaVie, the How to Recruit Doctors book is a must! This script book below is only for the experienced networker.

MLM Script Treasury: Not Your Usual Network Marketing Phone Scripts

http://www.amazon.com/Treasury-Network-Marketing-Scripts-ebook/dp/B00CKC5F38

MLM SCRIPT
TREASURY
NOT YOUR USUAL
NETWORK
MARKETING
PHONE
SCRIPTS

DAVID
WILLIAMS

By David Williams

Just released!

What is MonaVie? What is Acai Berry? Miracle or Sham?

89

This book is full of the top pulling, most valuable and very rare MLM phone scripts that have earned their users many hundreds of thousands of dollars. I will say right now, the material in this book is NOT 'newbie' friendly. These scripts are for pros. If you don't know what you're doing this book is not for you.

-Turn your prospects voice mail into a recruiting machine! 12 scripts which you can customize

-What do I say to make sure my prospects watch's my DVD or online presentation?

-What is a GAP line and why you should use one, and what to say on it.

-How to take your prospects pulse

-Top Tier Phone scripts – rare and valuable – and great to modify for your own phone scripts

-What to say to get your prospect on to a conference call

-How to close your prospect after a conference call – lots of trial closes, hard closes, and objection handlers

-Common objections and how to turn them back into closing questions

I have chosen scripts that I know you will NOT find in other script books for sale, or the free PDFs that float all over the Internet. The scripts contained here are the kind of scripts that only the top leaders in a program have access to and it usually requires someone to be invited to join their inner team to gain access to them.

This book is full of very hard hitting powerful scripts that have been used by many top prospectors and closers. You can use this book to build your own scripts by modifying what you find here.

-Scripts to get a prospect to commit to a live conference call

-The hardest closing questions from the industry

-Ads that will get your Voice Mail full, and what to say on your Voice Mail screener – lots of screeners and out bound messages

-What to say to your prospect AFTER the conference call

-Voice Scripts to 'wake up the dead' – get your inactive distributors active again

-Starting your own MLM or Team Call? Need a conference call script? – 4 full conference call scripts inside

-Are you a company trainer? Do you do many trainings? Are your people dying on the phone?

If you are a trainer, a serious upline, on your way to being a player, a 'big dog', this book is for you. If you are putting together your own scripts, calls, establishing your own team, or your own network marketing company – invest in this book. Inside this book you will find: hard hitting, hard closing power calls, what to say when you reach a prospects voice mail, screeners, actual company conference calls, GAP line messages and some special bonuses to get your phone ringing plus much, much more. It's all here.

What is in this book can take a serious player to the next level.

This is most definitely an 'insider's book'.

Williams latest book:

http://www.amazon.com/Autoresponder-Messages-Network-Marketing-ebook/dp/B00D38WD38

This book contains a professionally written email drip campaign of 30 powerful, engaging and entertaining persuasive email/autoresponder messages focused on your prospects 'Financial Woes' and how YOU can help your prospect solve them.

Warning!

If you have been in Network Marketing for any length of time, you probably have accumulated a list of prospects and their email address. However, many of these pro-spects have entered the 'witness protection program'. In other words, they never call back or reply to your emails. Most people forget about this list, but there is GOLD in it!

Now, you probably have an email system you pay for that is filled with 'canned' autoresponders about your company, or even some generic versions to send to your list. Sometimes this is part of your 'backoffice'.

But, have you read these autoresponders being sent in your name?

They suck.

Here's why:

You have a prospect who is looking to solve THEIR problem, which is lack of money. They need money, income, some light at the end of the tunnel, cash, maybe some dough to save their home... BUT they are NOT shopping for a MLM company, an INDUSTRY, or how long your company has been in business, or even what your product does...NO... they are desperate for a SOLUTION to their problems!

But if all the emails you send out are about 'the company, the timing, the industry...or how someone else is making money – no wonder they don't bother responding to you!

Can you imagine sending emails to starving children with stories about the kids in your family that have so much food... that they're fat? Of course not. So why send emails to financially struggling people about how others are rich?

Your prospect doesn't care about other people's wealth when THEY are broke and in financial pain. In fact, it works the other why. Resentment, suspicion, distrust.

Their mind is on their lack of money and they are worried.

They are awake all night worrying about their debt because they are in financial trouble.

And what? You send them an email about how old your company is?

It's basic marketing folks; offer your prospect a solution to their problem, and relate to them on their terms.

At this point, all your prospect is interested in is finding 'a way to earn money'.

NOTE *** If you are new and have not earned a re-spectable income, chances are your upline will tell you to borrow someone else's story, but doing that only begs the question from your prospect– 'well, if every-one else is making money in your company, why aren't you?'

Forget that.

So, what is in this book? Do I teach you how to write emails? NO…NO…and NO!!!!

Is this some lessons on basic copy writing for MLM? Heck NO!!!

But let's face it. Most people can't write a note to save their lives, let alone a well-crafted email campaign. Forget learning a skill that will take you years to master – just use expert messages instead!

That's where this book of powerful 'financial woes' autoresponder messages will come to your aid.

Inside are 30 rock solid emails that focus on your prospects financial situation - with engaging humor and playfulness - showing how YOU and your program can help him out of his or her financial mess.

FULL DISCLOUSER – this is a small book – 30 powerful emails. You are not paying for the quantity of words, you are paying for the quality of the message and for getting your phone to ring.

This book contains 30 well-crafted powerfully written emails that and fun and engaging that will suggest and reinforce to your prospect that YOU are the answer to their financial problems using proven psychological and persuasion techniques.

Take these email autoresponder messages and enter them into your backoffice or your email program. Start dripping on your list with these professionally written email messages – each crafted to have your prospect motivated to reach out and call YOU as an answer to their Financial Woes!

OVER

150

THE
SIMPLEST,
SHORTEST,
MOST
POWERFUL MLM AND
NETWORK MARKETING
PROSPECT CONTROL
AND CLOSING LINES
AND SCRIPTS, EVER.

DAVID
WILLIAMS

http://www.amazon.com/Network-Marketing-Online-Professional-ebook/dp/B00DVCTK78

Do you have trouble closing prospects? Do you feel you lose control of your prospecting and follow up calls? Do you have trouble closing strong prospects – the very ones you desperately want on your team?

Well, this book is for you. It's the lowest price but highest value book on Amazon. Why? Because this little book contains over 120 of the strongest, easiest, subtlest closing and 'keeping control' and 'taking control' over the conversation lines for network marketers.

FULL DISCLOSURE: This is a short book. This book has over 150 'lines'; mostly one line sentences. But don't be fooled by the size of the book. These are powerful closing lines to allow you to close your prospect. This is NOT a book on prospecting, recruiting or even a script book.

This is a book that should be open at your desk as you make your prospecting and follow up calls. If you find you prospect off their script (they never stay on script – only you can do that), these lines will bring you back into control.

They are subtle, but powerful. Here's some samples:

How much does it cost?
Millions of dollars not to get involved

Can you see yourself taking people through a process just like I did with you?

You can't outsource your learning

The table's set

This is thick

I'm not claiming we have an automatic system, I'm demonstrating it

Get into the game with us

Let me layout how the business will start for you

This is just a process to see if there a fit for you

This is not a pressure gig

It's just the way we do this (process)

There's no glory in paying bills

I promise I'm not going to push you, chase you or sell you

I'm not going to come back to close you, but to personalize the business for you

NOTE: with very little modification, you can use many of these lines as ad headers, email subject lines, or as smart and directed text in emails or create new phone scripts or reinvigorate old ones.

Now, you don't have to memorize these lines, you just need to have your Kindle reader, iPad or even your Kindle for PC open, (or you can print out the pages), when you are making your calls. If you lose control of a conversation, or have a strong person on the line (the best kind to recruit), these 'lines' are the arrows in your quiver.

Make these lines your own. They have been collected by professionals and have earned those who have used them millions of dollars, no exaggerating, millions of dollars. Now for .99 cents they are yours.

This book of powerful network marketing closing and control lines provides you with the easiest way to sound strong on the phone. You just need to use them. You need to sound strong. Your prospect will never know what hit them until you are training them, and tell them to pick up this little book.

If they won't spend .99 cents, to get a copy, they aren't worth your time. If they ask you to make them a copy instead, they have just told you they are not worth your time. You now own this book, make these lines your own, become powerful and rich.

You do deserve it!